Barnard Environmental Magnet School
170 Derby Avenue
New Haven, CT 06511

JAPAN
the culture

Bobbie Kalman

A Bobbie Kalman Book

The Lands, Peoples, and Cultures Series

Crabtree Publishing Company
www.crabtreebooks.com

The Lands, Peoples, and Cultures Series
Created by Bobbie Kalman
For baby Eloise

Author: Bobbie Kalman

Revised edition: Plan B Book Packagers

Coordinating editor: Ellen Rodger

Copy editor: Adrianna Morganelli

Proofreader: Crystal Sikkens

Project editor: Robert Walker

Production coordinator: Katherine Kantor

Editors/first edition:
Janine Schaub
Christine Arthurs
Margaret Hoogeveen
Jane Lewis

Photographs:
7382489561/Shutterstock Inc.: cover; Claudia Aaldijk/ Shutterstock Inc.: p. 11 (bottom right); Henrik Andersen/ Shutterstock Inc.: p. 13 (top); Alexey Averiyanov/ Shutterstock Inc.: p. 30 (bottom); Ryan Bouie/Shutterstock Inc.: p. 17 (top); Rachelle Burnside/ Shutterstock Inc.: p. 12 (top); Sam DCruz/Shutterstock Inc.: p 5, 8 (bottom); Fukuoka Irina/Shutterstock Inc.: p. 16 (bottom); Courtesy of Japan National Tourist Organization: p. 10, 20 (top), 21 (bottom), 22 (top), 23 (bottom); Katariina Järvinen/Shutterstock Inc.: p. 11 (bottom left); John Leung/Shutterstock Inc.: p. 4, 23 (top); Jenny Mie Lau King/Shutterstock Inc.: p. 19; koi88/Shutterstock Inc.: p 27, 29 (bottom); Joan Mann/ Cameramann Int'l., Ltd.: p. 3, 9 (both), 14 (bottom), 18 (top), 24, 26;

Christine McClymont: p. 20 (bottom); Chris McCooey/Shutterstock Inc.: p. 13 (bottom); Martin Mette/Shutterstock Inc.: p. 29 (top); Phaif/ Shutterstock Inc.: p. 8 (top); Radu Razvan/ Shutterstock Inc.: p. 7 (top left), 16 (top), 30 (top); Tristan Scholze/Shutterstock Inc.: p. 6 (top), 17 (bottom); Daniel P. Shibilski/Shutterstock Inc.: p. 28; Elias Wakan/Pacific Rim Slide Bank: p. 6 (bottom), 25 (top left); Naomi Wakan/Pacific Rim Slide Bank: p. 25 (bottom); Brian Weed/Shutterstock Inc.: p. 25 (top right); Jamie Worling: p. 14 (top), 15; Michael S. Yamashita/Corbis: p. 12 (bottom), 21 (top), 31 (top); Zaporozhchenko Yury/Shutterstock Inc.: p. 7 (top right), 18 (bottom); Olga Zaporozhskaya/ Shutterstock Inc.: title page.

Every effort has been made to obtain the appropriate credit and full copyright clearance for all images in this book. Any oversights, or omissions, will be corrected in future editions.

Illustrations:
Dianne Eastman: icons
David Wysotski, Allure Illustrations: back cover

Cover: get image choice from Crabtree.

Title page: Dancers in traditional dress perform at a festival on Okinawa, a Japanese island.

Icon: Torii gates

Back cover: Red-faced Japanese snow monkeys earned their name by surviving in areas with harsh winters.

Library and Archives Canada Cataloguing in Publication

Kalman, Bobbie, 1947-
    Japan : the culture / Bobbie Kalman. -- Rev. ed.

(The lands, peoples, and cultures series)
Includes index.
ISBN 978-0-7787-9298-7 (bound).--ISBN 978-0-7787-9666-4 (pbk.)

    1. Japan--Social life and customs--1945- --Juvenile literature.
I. Title. II. Series: Lands, peoples, and cultures series

DS821.K3 2008   j952   C2008-903481-3

Library of Congress Cataloging-in-Publication Data

Kalman, Bobbie.
    Japan the culture / Bobbie Kalman. -- Rev. ed.
        p. cm. -- (The lands, peoples, and cultures series)
    "A Bobbie Kalman book."
    Includes index.
    ISBN-13: 978-0-7787-9666-4 (pbk. : alk. paper)
    ISBN-10: 0-7787-9666-3 (pbk. : alk. paper)
    ISBN-13: 978-0-7787-9298-7 (reinforced library binding : alk. paper)
    ISBN-10: 0-7787-9298-6 (reinforced library binding : alk. paper)
    1. Japan--Civilization--1945---Juvenile literature. I. Title.
DS822.5.K235 2008
952--dc22
                                                        2008023521

Crabtree Publishing Company

www.crabtreebooks.com   1-800-387-7650

Published in Canada
Crabtree Publishing
616 Welland Ave.
St. Catharines, ON
L2M 5V6

Published in the United States
Crabtree Publishing
PMB16A
350 Fifth Ave., Suite 3308
New York, NY 10118

Published in the United Kingdom
Crabtree Publishing
White Cross Mills
High Town, Lancaster
LA1 4XS

Published in Australia
Crabtree Publishing
386 Mt. Alexander Rd.
Ascot Vale (Melbourne)
VIC 3032

Contents

Living in Japan is like being part of two contrasting worlds. Modern Japan is an **industrialized** nation of skyscrapers, busy highways, and the newest high-tech products. Japanese people dress in the latest styles and use modern products and technology. The other Japan is a country deeply rooted in its past. It is a traditional world influenced by a love of art, nature, beauty, and **ritual**.

Many Japanese come from a common background, so they share many of the same values, beliefs, and customs. There are many fascinating rituals, traditions, and celebrations to discover in Japan.

(opposite page) A dancer performs in traditional clothing for the opening of a modern grocery store.

(right) Tokyo is known for its bright and modern shopping districts, where neon signs and heavy traffic are common.

(below) Worshipers pray at a temple in Okinawa.

Nature is an important theme in Japanese **culture**. Its beauty and harmony have inspired poets, painters, and musicians. Many Japanese customs and festivals highlight nature's endless cycles. The Japanese celebrate every change the seasons bring. In spring, people rejoice at the arrival of new flowers, and in autumn they delight in the spectacular colors of the leaves. In winter people go to quiet, snow-covered parks and forests to view the snow.

Cherry blossom viewing

For fifty-one weeks of the year the cherry trees in Japan look ordinary. When they bloom for one week in spring, however, everyone celebrates. People watch the news eagerly to find out the locations of the best viewing spots. Thousands of picnickers gather under branches covered with pink and white flowers. These picnics, or flower viewing parties, are called *hanami*. The blossoms are at their peak for only a day or two and then they are gone for another year.

(right) A hanami *party gathers to enjoy the cherry blossoms.*

Bonsai

Bonsai, which is the art of raising miniature trees, is more than a thousand years old. Dwarfed trees are planted in pots and the branches and roots are constantly pruned to restrict their growth. Many *bonsai* trees are handed down from one **generation** to the next.

(left) Some bonsai trees have belonged to one family for many generations and are extremely valuable.

Sculpted gardens

Japanese gardens are works of art. Wherever there is space, people plant gardens. Instead of lawns and flower beds, Japanese gardens contain rocks, pebbles, sand, trees, ponds, and running water. These elements create a miniature world. Rocks represent mountains, a pond is a tiny ocean, trees **symbolize** a forest, and a running stream of water reminds people of a river. In many homes, a sliding door opens onto a carefully tended garden. Framed by the doorway, the garden is a living picture.

The beauty of wood

Wood is admired for its natural beauty, its fragrant scent, and its warmth. The Japanese say that a tree has two lives: one while it is growing and another when it has been made into a useful object. Instead of being painted, walls and floors are stained or **varnished** to preserve the wood's natural qualities.

Preserving nature

Despite the love that individuals feel toward nature, the Japanese as a society have not treated their environment with care. Rapid industrialization has caused a great deal of pollution. The Japanese people have taken some steps to solve their environmental problems, but it is a huge job. One of Japan's most challenging tasks is to clean up and preserve the environment that has brought its people so much pleasure.

(above left and right) Gardens are meant to be admired from a distance. The trees, rocks, and water inspire feelings of peace in the viewer.

7

Over the centuries, Japanese artists have developed unique styles of sculpture, painting, and **ceramics**. In addition to these arts, the Japanese also specialize in a whole range of crafts that they have developed into fine arts.

Painting with ink

A long time ago, Japanese culture was greatly influenced by the Chinese. It is not surprising, then, that early Japanese and Chinese painting styles are both based on the brush strokes of **calligraphy**. Japanese ink painting, or *sumi-e*, illustrates an object in just a few brush strokes. Every stroke is crucial to the painting. Like many other Japanese **art forms**, *sumi-e* has strict rules. For example, students must learn how to paint grass before they can paint the more complicated cherry blossom.

Origami

Origami is the Japanese art of folding paper into objects without cutting or pasting. Squares of brightly colored or patterned paper are made specifically for *origami*. This crisp paper holds the sharp folds *origami* requires. A single piece of paper can be folded into the shape of a flower, fish, bird, or animal. An *origami* artist can create animals that move, such as a bird that flaps its wings when its tail is pulled, or a frog that hops when its back is tapped.

(top) Origami *ranges from simple designs to complex folded paper works of art.*

(bottom left) *An artist sells his calligraphy on the street.*

Handmade paper

Washi is the Japanese word for handmade paper. Many people call it "rice paper," but it is not made from rice. The inner bark from three kinds of plants is pounded into mush and mixed with a solution to produce a thick, pasty substance (shown right). This paste is spread onto bamboo mesh screens. When it has dried, sheets of paper are carefully pulled off the screens. Delicately patterned *washi* makes excellent gift wrap.

One-of-a-kind ceramic cups

Irregularly shaped, hand-molded ceramic cups are among the most prized pieces of pottery in Japan. Cups made by **master** potters are cherished for their usefulness and beauty. People admire them for such natural characteristics as a potter's fingerprint in the clay, a bubble in the glaze, an uneven edge, or a dent in the shape. The beauty of these one-of-a-kind cups is meant to be experienced by touch as well as sight.

(below) Japan has many different styles, or traditions, of pottery and pottery making.

The treasures of Japan

Masters of traditional art forms such as paper making, *sumi-e* painting, and pottery are respected for their skills, dedication, and for the beautiful works they create.

Living treasures

Thousands of Japanese people are skilled in the traditional arts. Only a small number of them, however, receive the great honor of being named a "Living National Treasure." This title is reserved for the very best artists. Living National Treasures receive money from the government so they can continue their work. The award is intended as an honor that ensures that they will pass on their valuable skills to the next generation. Dedicated **apprentices** study for many years learning the techniques of the Living National Treasures. The goal is to help younger artists learn from masters to preserve techniques, build upon style, and create new works of art.

Kokeshi dolls

Wooden *kokeshi* dolls have long, slender bodies with large, round heads. After delicate facial features and flower designs are painted on the plain wood, the dolls are coated with a shiny finish. *Kokeshi* dolls are prized by doll lovers all over the world.

(opposite page) This artisan is hard at work carving a wooden mask. Turn the page to find out more about this type of mask.

Story paintings

About nine hundred years ago, Japanese artists began making story paintings on scrolls. Unlike *sumi-e* paintings, story paintings are colorful and extremely detailed. The most famous are scenes from a novel called *The Tale of Genji.* This novel, written by a noblewoman named Lady Murasaki, recounts the life of a prince.

(above) This artist is painting Japanese caricatures. The style of illustration was introduced by an artist named Jusaburo Sharaku. In 1794, he made over one hundred prints of actors, which are now famous worldwide.

(below) Kokeshi dolls are delicate and beautiful works of art.

According to Japanese **mythology**, theater was first discovered by the gods. The gods then passed on their knowledge to the Japanese. Over the centuries, Japanese theater has developed into several rich traditions.

Noh theater

Noh is Japan's oldest form of theater. Performances date back to the 1300s and 1400s when plays were put on for the *samurai* and upper classes. *Noh* theater is still performed today. The most famous plays are based on legends and folktales. *Noh* plays often have a dream-like quality and feature ghosts and spirits. The plays teach that life is like a wheel and that good and bad fortune come and go in a never-ending cycle. *Noh* theater is well known for its masks and spectacular costumes. The two main characters change their masks frequently to reveal different emotions. If the heroine is miserable, she wears a mask to show her sadness. When she feels better, she puts on a happy mask. The scenery of a *Noh* play is simple; sometimes the stage is almost bare.

(right) A wooden Noh *mask.*

(below) Bunraku *puppeteers work in full view of the audience, but the audience soon forgets about them because all attention is focused on the life-like puppets.*

Bunraku puppets

Bunraku is a musical puppet theater for adults. *Bunraku* puppets are almost as big as real people. Clothed in black, the puppeteers stand on stage behind the puppets. It takes three skillful puppeteers to work a *Bunraku* puppet: one for the body and right arm, one for the left arm, and one for the feet. A narrator, called a *tayu*, tells the story and speaks the puppets' lines. Music from a stringed instrument called a *samisen* accompanies the action.

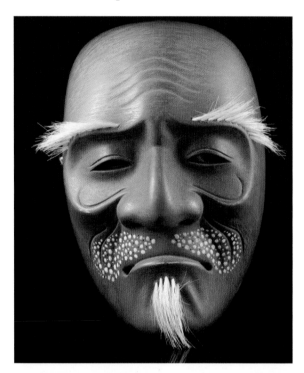

Kabuki

Kabuki theater is also very old. It was created in the early 1600s. *Kabuki* was started by a woman and was originally performed by women actors. Today, men play all the parts, including the women's roles.

For many people, a *kabuki* play is a social occasion. It is acceptable for members of the audience to make noise and voice their opinions during the performance. People bring their own food and eat while they enjoy the show. *Kabuki* performances can be quite long—some last up to six-and-a-half hours!

Kabuki theater was originally performed for the lower classes. The plays use humor to teach a lesson. They are often about ordinary people outsmarting members of the upper classes.

An orchestra, **chorus**, and dancers are all part of a *kabuki* play. The chorus sings the story while the performers act out their parts. The actors wear elaborate costumes and heavy makeup, and use exaggerated gestures.

(above) Kabuki *plays were originally for ordinary people, but are now performed at the National Theater of Japan.*

(below) The Minamuzi Theater is located in Kyoto.

Shinto and Buddhism

Japan has two main religions: Shinto and Buddhism. Both have had a tremendous effect on Japanese culture. Religious and non-religious people alike are influenced by the ideas and rituals of these religions.

Shinto

The Shinto religion is the original religion of the Japanese. Shinto means "the way of the gods." Japanese people believe that gods and goddesses called *kami* dwell in natural structures such as rocks, trees, plants, waterfalls, and animals. There are also *kami* that protect people from earthquakes, diseases, and fires. The most important *kami* is Amaterasu, the sun goddess. She is the symbol of Japan, and it is believed that all the emperors descended from her.

Those who practice Shinto believe that all living things share the same life source. Shinto teaches respect for nature. It also encourages family members to fulfill the hopes of their **ancestors** and honor the heroes of the past.

Shinto shrines

Shinto **shrines** are usually built in beautiful settings where worshipers can appreciate nature and feel close to the gods and the spirits of their ancestors. Weddings and baby-blessing ceremonies take place at Shinto shrines. Local shrines honor the *kami* that protect villages and communities. Besides visiting neighborhood shrines, the Japanese also take trips to major Shinto shrines. The most **sacred** shrine in Japan, located in Ise, is dedicated to Amaterasu.

Japanese people believe that *torii* gates serve as entrances to the spiritual world. These wooden arches are a common sight at Shinto shrines and can also be found in picturesque spots all by themselves. *Torii* gates act as frames through which nature's beauty can be appreciated.

(above) When entering a Buddhist temple, people light an incense stick, strike a metal gong, place their hands together, and bow.

(left) Before entering a Shinto shrine, worshipers rinse their mouths and pour water onto their fingertips as acts of purification.

Buddhism

Buddhism is an ancient religion that originally came from India. It spread through China and Korea and eventually came to Japan in the sixth century. Buddhism is based on the teachings of a man named Sakyamuni who became known as the "Enlightened One," or Buddha.

Buddhists believe that people are born over and over again and that all their actions have an effect on their next lives. If a person lives a good life, he or she will be rewarded with a better one the next time around. Japanese people practice ancestor worship. Many homes have small Buddhist altars with photographs of deceased family members.

Zen and *zazen*

There are several kinds of Buddhism. Since the 1100s, the most popular form in Japan has been Zen Buddhism. Zen Buddhism stresses **meditation** as the way of letting the mind become quiet and experiencing the mysteries of life. Zen Buddhists practice a kind of meditation called *zazen*. The purpose of *zazen* is to clear the mind of any thoughts and attachments. To help them meditate, Buddhists sit in the lotus position—back straight, chin tucked in, and legs crossed with the soles of their feet facing upward. Priests and monks often face the wall while meditating so that there are fewer distractions. Meditation sessions can last for many hours at a time.

Built in 1252, the Amida Buddha is over forty-six feet (14 m) high. The wooden building that once housed the statue was swept away by a tsunami, which is a huge wave caused by an earthquake under the sea.

(top) Men dressed in traditional battle suits prepare to reenact a scene from a famous clan battle during a festival in Yonezawa City.

(bottom left) An archer on horseback competes in a festival honoring Japan's ancient past.

Japan has many festivals, called *matsuri*. They include lively parades, competitions, games, and music. Many Japanese festivals celebrate the planting, growing, and harvesting of rice. Others honor ancestors, children, or the changing of the seasons.

The Festival of Ages

The Festival of Ages, or *Jidai Matsuri*, is held at Heian Shrine in Kyoto. From the year 794 to 1185, Kyoto was the capital of Japan. *Jidai Matsuri* celebrates the founding of this ancient capital. Everyone dresses in costumes from the past. Women wear colorful silk **kimonos** from different time periods. People dress up as royalty, armored *samurai*, and rice farmers and march through the streets of Kyoto. Even the horses are decorated!

A festival of lanterns

One of the bigger festivals in Japan is the *Bon* Festival, also known as the Festival of the Dead. The *Bon* Festival honors ancestors. Japanese people believe that the spirits of their dead relatives visit them every year for four days in July. On one night of the festival, family members gather from all over the country and join together in prayer at the family grave site. On another night, people celebrate the return of the spirits by dancing under rows of brightly colored lanterns outside Buddhist temples. The participants, dressed in light summer kimonos called *yakata*, follow the movements of a group of lead dancers. The dance is meant to welcome and entertain the spirits of the ancestors. As the people dance in a counterclockwise direction, they resemble a giant human wheel. The wheel represents the Buddhist belief in reincarnation, or that life is a cycle in which death follows life and rebirth follows death.

(top) A woman with the white makeup of a young geisha, performs at a traditional festival.

(bottom) A team competes in the Yamakasa, a festival in Fukuoka that is over 700 years old! Teams of men wearing loincloths called shimekomi, race against other teams, all carrying heavy floats.

Festivals throughout the year

There are festivals during every season in Japan. The year begins with the biggest celebration of all—New Year. People start preparing for the New Year early in December. They pay off debts, clean their homes, and put up decorations. They buy new clothes for themselves and gifts for their friends. At midnight on New Year's Eve, the ropes of the giant bells at the Buddhist temples are pulled 108 times to ring out 108 sins. Many people visit Shinto shrines during the first week of the year.

New Year's Day is like a giant birthday party because everyone adds a year to his or her age. People eat a special breakfast and dress in their best clothes. Everyone opens New Year cards. Children receive gifts of money. The day is reserved for visiting family and friends.

(right) These people are tying paper fortunes on a string at the shrine to ensure that their wishes will come true in the coming year.

(below) Crowds of people visit a Shinto shrine on New Year's Day.

New Year decorations

Pine, bamboo, and rope are used in New Year decorations. Pine stands for long life, and bamboo represents flexibility. Rope is a symbol of the sun goddess, Amaterasu. According to legend, Amaterasu hid in a cave after her brother, the wind god, destroyed her rice fields. The sun disappeared from the sky, and the whole world was thrown into darkness. Eight million gods and goddesses gathered outside the cave with a plan to lure out Amaterasu. They began singing and dancing. When the sun goddess poked her head out to see what was going on, the gods grabbed her. They placed a rope over the entrance of the cave. At New Year, ropes hang at the entrances of Shinto shrines and decorate homes.

Women perform the flower hat dance at a cherry blossom festival.

Festive flying

In spring, people put a great deal of time and effort into making large, colorful kites. Some are so large that they need to be controlled by many people holding several strings. The best place to see spectacular kites is in Nagasaki, where there is a giant kite festival every April. Kite-flying competitions are held in which competitors try to keep their kites in the air while others try to knock them down with their kites.

Summer festivals

Many Japanese festivals are held in the summer. During the warm weather, outdoor celebrations include climbing poles, racing boats, walking in **processions**, playing tug-of-war, dancing, and singing. At night, people carry lanterns or torches and parade through the darkness. During *Gion Matsuri*, the most important summer festival, a parade of fantastic floats on giant wooden wheels winds its way through the city of Kyoto.

The Japanese also celebrate winter festivals such as *Yuki Matsuri* and *Kamakura*. *Setsubun* celebrates the end of winter.

A winter carnival

Sapporo is the capital city of Hokkaido, an island in northern Japan. On the first day of February, residents hold a snow festival called *Yuki Matsuri*. Trucks transport thousands of loads of snow to the main square. Huge blocks of ice are cut from frozen rivers nearby and hauled to the site. More than two thousand people work together to create massive ice sculptures. People from all over visit Sapporo to see the ice sculptures and exciting parades.

(above and below) During Yuki Matsuri, people carve blocks of ice into figures of famous people, animals, Buddhas, spaceships, and well-known buildings.

Kamakura

Kamakura, meaning "snow hut," is celebrated in the town of Yokote. With the help of their parents, girls hollow out huge snowdrifts like igloos. They cover the floor with a thick straw mat called a **tatami** and place lighted candles on a shelf that has been carved into the wall. The girls leave their shoes outside, sit on the mat in socks and slippers, and wrap themselves in warm quilts. They heat rice cakes over a small charcoal stove. Parents and neighbors come to visit. The girls offer their guests rice cakes and tea or rice wine. The visitors leave fruit and coins in return. Sometimes the girls are allowed to spend the night in their *kamakura*.

Setsubun

Setsubun takes place on February 3. It is a bean-throwing festival. The Japanese throw beans to frighten away winter spirits, therefore allowing spring spirits to return. Although the Japanese love winter, they look forward to the beautiful blossoms and warm weather of spring.

(above) During the four-day winter carnival of Yuki Matsuri, *people ski and skate and have all kinds of winter fun.*

(below) These girls keep warm by wearing thick kimonos and huddling near a charcoal stove. They have received several pieces of fruit and some coins from family and friends.

21

⛩ Festivals for the young ⛩

The Japanese honor their children by setting aside several days of the year just for them. The numbers three, five, and seven are considered lucky numbers, and are part of these festivals.

The *Shichi-go-san* Festival

Shichi means seven, *go* means five, and *san* means three. If you were seven, five, or three years old in Japan, you would look forward to November 15. It is a day of celebration for children of these ages. On the day of *Shichi-go-san*, children dress in traditional clothes. Boys wear wide trousers called *hakama*, and girls wear kimonos. Families go to local shrines and pray to their patron *kami* for the good health of the children. The children ring a giant bell and clap their hands to get the attention of the *kami*, and then they recite a brief prayer. Afterward, the children receive many presents at parties with family and friends. *Shichi-go-san* is a lot like a birthday party!

Hina Matsuri

Girls look forward to *Hina Matsuri*, or the Doll Festival, on March 3, which is the third day of the third month. Girls dress in their best kimonos and display their family's collection of historical dolls. The dolls represent members of the royal family. The emperor and empress are set at the top of the display, while other members of the noble class are on lower steps. The dolls are valuable works of art, with delicate features and beautiful silk clothes. Some are several hundred years old. The display also includes tiny furniture and dishes with treats for the dolls. Peach blossoms, a symbol of beauty, decorate the sides of the display. Family and friends come to view the dolls. The young hosts offer their guests tea and cakes.

These young girls are dressed in their best kimonos for Shichi-go-san.

Children's Day

Children's Day is held on May 5, the fifth day of the fifth month. The carp and the iris are the symbols for this festival. Both represent strength and courage and remind children to face life's challenges with determination. The carp is a symbol of strength because it must swim upriver against the current to lay its eggs. The leaves of the iris are as sharp as the swords used by courageous *samurai* warriors of the past. Boys proudly display *samurai* armor, swords, and warrior dolls. Carp made of paper or cloth are hung on bamboo poles outside every home. One carp is hung for each family member.

The *Tanabata* Festival

The *Tanabata* Festival is held on July 7, the seventh day of the seventh month. It celebrates two stars, the Weaver Princess and the Shepherd, who fell in love and were punished for neglecting their heavenly duties. They were separated by the **Milky Way** and were only allowed to meet on this one day each year. In honor of the stars, young people parade through the streets carrying lanterns, colorful streamers, and bamboo poles decorated with strips of paper on which love poems have been written.

Coming of Age

Coming of Age Day, or *Seijin shiki*, is a big deal in Japan. Held each year on the second Monday of January, it marks a young person's passage into adulthood. The day includes ceremonies and parties for family and friends. Young people who turn 20 during the year dress up in traditional or formal wear. Young women wear kimonos and *furisode*, or long draped sleeves and fur collars. Young men wear suits or traditional dark kimonos.

(left) A young girl admires one of her friend's priceless dolls for Hina Matsuri.

(top) Young women in kimonos and fur collars celebrate Coming of Age day.

🏯 Ancient robes 🏯

For 2,000 years, Japanese men, women, girls, and boys have worn kimonos. The kimono is a floor-length silk robe **embroidered** with intricate designs. The most complicated designs are woven on hand-operated looms. This garment, which has no buttons or zippers, is held together by a sash at the waist.

Seasonal kimonos

Most kimonos are made in a standard size, style, and cut. They differ only in color and quality. Light, comfortable kimonos called *yukata* are worn in summer, and cozy, flannel kimonos called *nemaki* are worn in winter. There are formal kimonos in dark colors for men, and bright, embroidered kimonos for women.

How to put on a kimono

The formal women's kimono is the most difficult to put on. The first layer is a slip called a *nagajuban*. *Tabi*, which are socks that separate the big toe from the other toes, are put on at the same time. The outer kimono, which is made of heavier silk, comes next. It has sleeves that hang down to the ground. The kimono is always folded with the left side over the right. Instead of a sash, a woman wears an *obi*, which is a wide band of embroidered silk that wraps tightly around her waist. A woman in a kimono may look beautiful, but she is not comfortable. It is difficult to breathe, lift her arms, bend over, or take normal-sized steps.

These girls are dressed up for a festival.

(above left) This ancient kimono, displayed on a mannequin, has twelve layers. Kamon, or family crests, are part of the pattern.

(above right) When a woman is dressed in her best kimono, she usually wears a beautiful hairstyle to complement her outfit.

(right) On festival days boys often wear wide-legged trousers called hakama.

There is much more involved in a Japanese tea ceremony than just drinking a cup of tea. It is a ritual that involves a series of actions carried out in simple and quiet surroundings. It takes many years to master the art of making, serving, and taking Japanese tea correctly.

A long tea-drinking tradition

Tea drinking in Japan dates back to the **Middle Ages** when the Japanese were introduced to tea by the Chinese. At first, tea was used by Zen priests to help them stay awake during meditation. Over the centuries, rules were developed for carrying out the tea ceremony.

The tea ceremony is still a popular ritual. It teaches people about Japanese culture and helps them think in a disciplined way. Some people say that learning the tea ceremony is like learning the steps of a complicated and elegant dance. The host and guests concentrate throughout the long ceremony, and everyone involved knows in advance what they are expected to do.

A formal noontime tea

There are many variations of the Japanese tea ceremony. The way each one is performed depends on the occasion or time of day. A formal noontime tea ceremony is performed by a host for up to five guests. The guests are invited to a tea house surrounded by a garden. When they arrive, they must wait fifteen minutes in a small room near the garden gate. An attendant leads them to an outdoor waiting area. The host and guests greet one another with silent bows and walk together toward the tea room, admiring the gardens along the way. After cleansing their hands and removing their shoes, they file into the tea room through a small door. The last person shuts the door with a bang and locks it. This is a signal to the host that he or she may light the charcoal fire in the fire pit.

Preparing the tea

While the coals grow hot and the water in the kettle boils, the guests are served a small snack. After it is eaten, the host collects the dishes in silence. Keeping silent is meant to bring the feelings of the host and guests into harmony. The host mixes powdered tea with hot water to make a thick, green paste. The group holds a brief, formal conversation while sipping the tea. Each guest admires the beautiful cups and utensils. Then everyone is silent again, and the fire is smothered. A thin, frothy tea is served at the end, drawing the ceremony to a close.

(left) Tea sweets, called kashi *or* o-kashi, *are made from sweet potatoes and green tea powder.*

(opposite page) The tea is made with water that has been boiled in a kettle over a charcoal pit.

⛩ Geisha life ⛩

Geisha were once common sights on the streets of major Japanese cities such as Tokyo and Kyoto. Today, geisha are rarely seen outside of the areas where they live and train, called *hanamachi*. Geisha are female entertainers who dress in beautiful traditional kimonos. They also wear elaborate hairstyles and special makeup. Geisha are trained from an early age in music and dance. In the past, geisha entertained clients at geisha houses. Today, many geisha are hired to work at tea houses, traditional restaurants, and even in resort towns.

Geisha dress

Young or apprentice geisha are called *maiko*. *Maiko* wear a *furisode*, or traditional and formal kimonos made of many layers of brightly colored and patterned silk. The furisode has long swinging sleeves. They wear the kimono with an *obi*, or wide belt. On their feet they wear white socks with a split toe and high wooden sandals called *okobo*. *Maiko* also wear heavy white makeup. Mature geisha wear more demure but expensive kimonos, less makeup, and lower-heeled footwear.

Geisha are so much a part of Japanese popular culture, that there are geisha dolls and art.

White geisha makeup is applied to the face, neck, and shoulders. Geisha wear obi *tied in the back.*

Makeup and hair

Most geisha photos show the heavily made-up apprentice *maiko*. They traditionally wear a thick white base with red lips and red and black eye makeup. Except for special occasions, older geisha wear less makeup. Geisha hairstyles are complex and involved. There are at least one dozen different hairstyles, most of them a variation of a chignon, or upswept bun. Geisha used to sleep with their necks on wooden supports so that they would not wreck their hairstyles. Today, many geisha wear wigs instead and sleep on pillows.

Geisha houses

Geisha live in geisha houses called *okiya*. There, *maiko* learn how to be geisha from older geisha. They are trained to sing, dance, recite poetry, and play games and traditional instruments. Geisha apprentices also learn the proper way to serve tea at *okiya* and at the tea houses where they are hired to work. Many successful geisha live on their own, outside of the *okiya*.

Cultural customs

The Japanese have many customs that emphasize respect for nature and order in society. In Japan, people appreciate empty space and nature. As a small island nation, with a growing population, natural space is prized. The Japanese celebrate it in festivals, through the building of parks, and also in their art.

In Japanese painting, white space is as important as the painted areas. When a Japanese person admires a tree, he or she also admires the shapes and areas of sky among the branches. Nature, both in art and in life, is viewed as something that should be valued and appreciated. Art includes nature and does not try to gain power over it.

Respect for traditions

The Japanese have unwritten codes that govern behavior on everything from greeting people to eating and even bathing! Bowing is very important in Japanese culture. People bow on greeting, to show respect, and to apologize. The length of a bow, how deep it is, and who bows first are all signs of a person's status in society. Older people and people considered important are not expected to bow as deeply. If a person is apologizing, the bow is deep, long, and the head is lowered.

(top) A row of Buddhas with red caps.

(bottom right) A woman bows and prays in front of a Buddha statue, showing respect for herself and her faith.

30

Bowing is a respectful greeting.

Mealtime manners

In Japan, children learn to use chopsticks at an early age to eat food. They are taught to clear their plates and not take more than they can eat. Wasting food, especially rice, is considered bad manners, but lifting a bowl of soup or rice to your mouth is okay. In fact, since it wastes less food, it is considered polite!

Take your shoes off!

Since most Japanese homes have wooden floors, people take their shoes off when entering. Shoes are left by the door with the toes facing out. Slippers are often offered to guests to wear in the house. Guests are expected to wear socks in the slippers and not dirty the slippers. Guests in turn are treated to the bests seats in the house and given the best food and drinks.

An upside-down frown

Have you heard the expression, "A smile is just a frown turned upside down?" This saying is particularly true in Japan. When a person smiles, it is not always a sign of happiness. A smile is often used to hide other emotions such as embarrassment, confusion, or anger.

Belly to belly

Many people associate love with the heart. For the Japanese, however, the stomach is the center of the emotions. Instead of having "heart-to-heart" talks, the Japanese "open their stomachs" for a good conversation. To compliment a friend for being generous, someone might say, "You are potbellied." Potbellied does not mean a person is chubby. It means he or she is big-hearted.

Glossary

ancestors People from whom one is descended

apprentice A person who works for an artisan in order to learn a trade or art

art form Work that is especially beautiful or meaningful. Sword making is a Japanese art form

artisan A craftsperson or skilled worker

calligraphy The art of fine handwriting. In Japan, calligraphers use special ink, paper, and brushes

caricature A painting or drawing in which the features of the subject are exaggerated

ceramic A type of pottery that is baked at temperatures higher than 900°F (500°C)

chorus A group of people that sings or speaks together at the same time

culture The customs, beliefs, and arts of a distinct group of people

embroidery Intricate designs sewn with a needle and thread

generation People born at about the same time. Grandparents, parents, and children represent three generations

incense A substance that produces a sweet-smelling smoke when burned

industrialization The term used to describe a shift from an agricultural society to one that produces goods in factories

kami Japanese gods and goddesses

kimono A loose-fitting, wide-sleeved Japanese robe that is tied with a sash

master A person of great skill or ability; an expert

meditation The act of emptying the mind of all thoughts and attachments in order to achieve a state of inner peace

Middle Ages The time period from A.D. 500 to 1500

Milky Way A galaxy made up of more than one hundred billion stars, appearing as a bright white path across the sky. Our solar system is part of the Milky Way

mythology A collection of legends or stories that try to explain mysterious events or ideas

procession A group of people walking in lines as part of a ceremony. Processions are common in Japanese festivals

purification The act of becoming clean. Before entering a Shinto shrine, the Japanese purify themselves by washing their hands and rinsing their mouths

ritual A formal custom in which several steps are faithfully followed

sacred Holy

samurai The warriors who lived in ancient Japan

shrine A structure that is dedicated to a deity. Those who believe in Shinto visit shrines that are dedicated to spirits called *kami*

symbolize To represent or stand for something else

tatami A standard-sized mat woven from rice straw

temple A sacred house of worship. Buddhists visit temples to practice their religious rituals

varnish To apply a liquid substance to wood that, when dry, makes the wood appear glossy

Index

Printed in the U.S.A.